Preface

I am a lifelong resident of Akron, OH who had grand ideas of what I wanted to be when I grew up. As a child, I always wanted to be a stuntman. I had no ideas on how to achieve that dream, so I focused on something that would be easier to attain. Or so I thought it would be easier....

While I was in high school, I had plans to become an electrical engineer. This dream was short-lived, as I struggled with the advanced math necessary to follow this career path. Instead, I decided to do the next best thing- become a music teacher.

When I originally enlisted into the Army National Guard in January of 1987, I had every intention of making it a career and retiring after 20 years. During my initial enlistment, there were some significant life altering changes that affected the desired outcome.

In 1990, three years into my initial enlistment, I was hit with my fiancé breaking off our engagement; my mom passing away from cancer at age 39; getting re-engaged to my ex-fiancé; dropping out of college, and then trying to find a completely different career path. That is when I decided to join the family business as an electrician.

By the time I was in the final year of my 6-year enlistment (late 1992), I was not only beginning my new electrical apprenticeship, but I also got married in June of 1992 for the first time. In 1997, Pam and I had our first, and only child, Dylan.

All of these sudden changes in a quick few years really forced me to grow up quicker than anticipated. Most of my struggles in dealing with all of the adversity was to go out and drink socially with friends (this was a precursor to things to come).

Fast forward to 2022. I am now in me early 50's and on my second marriage. Pam and I only lasted 9 years and ended up getting a divorce in 2001. Sharon and I met soon afterwards and were married in August of 2002. We have been blessed with a wonderfully blended family that gave us four children (three girls and one boy). At the time of this writing, we are quickly coming up on our 20-year anniversary.

Table of Contents

Introduction

Coming home from a war zone is not as easy as people think it is. It is not a plug and play state of mind where you just fall back into your old life. It is a long journey back, even after you are home. No soldier has the same story or series of events in their lives or path home. This is mine.

I remember a briefing from the military before we left for Iraq that each and every soldier leaves a small part of them behind when they come home from a deployment. I didn't know how true this statement was until it affected me personally. It not only affected me, but my entire family.

As a believer in Jesus Christ, I have struggled with these issues and whether or not I still wanted to believe in the saving power of Christ. More on this later.

The intention is not to be a story about what happened during my time in Iraq (though I will need to share a few instances that were cause and effect type of situations), but it's an opportunity to share about my struggles and personal demons that have plagued me since returning home. At the time of this writing, I have now been home 10 years. Seems like a long time to many, but for me, it seems like it was last year at times. Here we go-

Way back in 1987, I enlisted into the Ohio Army National Guard at the age of 17. I did my required contract from January 1987 to January 1993 and decided to get out instead of making it a career. This was a decision that I regretted for many years afterwards. During the summer of 2005, while attending the local fair, I ran into a recruiter that had the same unit patch from my old unit. We chatted a bit and he caught me up on some of the guys that we had in common. He surprised me with the question of if I had ever considered reenlisting.

Of course, I did. I always regretted getting out. I had unfinished business due to the events of 9/11. So, in September of 2005, I reenlisted as a sergeant in the Army National Guard and was assigned to the 1484th Transportation Co. I was determined to do my part as a soldier.

Two years into my second enlistment, there were talks of a sister unit deploying to Iraq. Since the 1484th just got home in the spring of 2005 before I reenlisted, I knew my chances of getting selected to go to the 1483rd were fairly high. After long talks with my wife, Sharon, it was decided that I would just volunteer to transfer for the deployment. I wanted to do things, as much as possible, on my terms.

After the transfer and months of preparation at my new unit, the time had come to board the bus for Camp Atterbury, IN for our mobilization training. We got on the bus on July 5th, 2009. What a horrible July 4th that year.

In late September, we flew out from Indiana and landed in Kuwait. When we landed in Kuwait, it was 3am. I never experienced anything quite like this. You get off of the plane in the middle of the night and it's still 97 degrees outside. I never knew that the outside air could burn your eyeballs.

When you're 40 years old and deployed it's a different ballgame. Most of the soldiers were in their 20's and early 30's, so I didn't share much common ground with many of them. I spent a lot of time isolated because of this. Not by their choice, but because it just naturally happened. The other result of being one of the older members of the unit was the added expectations of responsibilities.

The Mental Stressors

Twice during our deployment in Iraq, we had soldiers who did things to put their personal lives at risk. These episodes were quite different from one another and occurred at separate times of our deployment, but they affected me because I was put in charge of their safety and to escort them to Germany. Landstuhl, Germany was the staging location for wounded or sick soldiers to process out of the war theater. This would normally be a 3–5-day process for doctor's appointments and scheduling flights back to the United States.

Being responsible for the safety and well-being of someone who isn't in their right frame of mind is taxing in and of itself, but when the military decides that they will be monitored 24/7 they mean 24/7.

I was accused at various times of abandoning our other soldiers and not going on convoys because I was trying to get out of the missions. That wasn't the case. After being in Iraq for 5 months, my mission was about to change. It became about the individual and not the platoon.

One of the privates that came from the 1484th with me decided that he was going to drink an entire bottle of Nyquil. This, obviously, was not a smart decision. It ended up putting him in the hospital on post in Taji, Iraq. Our First Sergeant, the top sergeant in our entire company, pulled me off of the rifle range that day to take care of him. The feeling was that we were from the same unit, and I was an NCO (non-commissioned officer) that had familiarity with the soldier. Trying to take your life is no laughing matter in any occupation, but in a combat zone this is unacceptable and grounds for sending you back to the States.

With our private who had issues, it took the unit a week to get transportation lined up for us to get him from Al Taji in Central

Iraq to Landstuhl, Germany. During that time, I was on a 12 on and 12 off schedule with another soldier to watch our soldier and not let him out of our sight. He couldn't even go to the bathroom alone.

Finally, we were taken to the airfield to get on a chopper to head to Balad, Iraq, then onto a C130 transport plane to Kuwait, then again up to Germany. Flying is not the most enjoyable thing in a war zone as you can potentially sit in a terminal for upwards of 72 hours waiting for approval to take off. You never knew when the flights would be cleared for takeoff, so there was no possibility of going anywhere on base for anything, including a comfortable bed. Fortunately, this time, we didn't have all of the delays and we arrived in Germany on schedule.

Once we arrived on base in Germany, as a psych escort, you still needed to be with your soldier at all times. This included going to Dr. visits in the hospital and completing the required checklist in order for the soldier to get on a flight back to the states. After four days of chasing him around, he was released from my custody, and I started the long trek back to Iraq (which was another four days' travel).

On a separate occasion, one of our staff sergeants couldn't manage the stress of deployment. He disappeared without a trace. The entire south side of Taji was on lockdown as we were doing a manhunt for him. Since he still had his rifle and ammunition, the outcome could be really disastrous if we didn't find him soon. We searched throughout the night and into the morning with no leads.

As the next group of searchers took over in the morning, he was eventually found on the north side of base with the Iraqis. Nobody knew who he was over there, especially since he pulled off all of his name tags and unit patches. Once again, I get the notification from our senior leadership that I'm making a second trip to Germany as a psych patient escort.

With our staff sergeant, we were routed differently. We went from Al Taji to Balad to Baghdad. Red air happened in Baghdad which delayed us that 72 hours. (Red air is the term used for sandstorms, or poor visibility that would delay flights from taking off or landing.) Remember when I said that they were to have 24/7 watch? Guess what happens when you're the only soldier with them? You don't get to go to sleep. You will actually get in a lot of trouble if you go to sleep, and they wander off.

I had to call back to the unit and explain that I needed another soldier to allow me to get a little sleep. They didn't believe me until a medical officer got on the phone with them. I was so exhausted at this point that I really didn't care what my unit thought about me calling in for additional help. It was about 20 hours later when the two soldiers sent as my relief arrived. I was never happier to lay my head on a pillow than that afternoon. I slept for an entire day.

After our 72-hour delay, we said our goodbye to my relief, and the staff sergeant and I boarded the C130 for Germany. Needless to say, I was more than thrilled when we boarded the plane for Germany as there were medics aboard who took over for the flight. Finally, a little more sleep and mental rest.

Each time we arrived in Germany at the military base, these soldiers were once again in my charge until they were either admitted to the hospital or flown back to the states. More days of little to no sleep. I remember the episode with our staff sergeant while we were in the barracks in Germany. He was sleeping in his bed, and I decided to go down to the basement and put a load of laundry in the washing machine. When I got back to our room on the third floor, he was nowhere to be found.

Panicked, I started searching the floors and the dayroom for him. He was nowhere to be found. How do I explain that I failed at my mission and lost a soldier?? Frantically, I again searched the building with no luck. My next step was to notify the cadre in charge of this situation. I made one last look around and there he was- sitting on his bed. He said he got lost coming back from the bathroom (which was sandwiched between our room and an adjacent room).

Once I released the soldiers over to the medical unit in Germany, it was time to start scheduling the flights back to Al Taji. Again, this process is slow and painful. Due to all of this mental and physical stress, I was exhausted. The Army chaplain (who was a Major) stopped by and ordered me to join him on the outing into the city to help me cope with my stress. Of course, I couldn't tell a ranking officer 'No.'

Now, word got back to other soldiers in Al Taji somehow about this outing and I was accused of taking a vacation while they were running convoy missions. This obviously put more of a rift between me and the other soldiers. Screw all of you!

Sandwiched in between all of this was my youngest daughter having marital issues. Things were bad, but what made it worse was that I couldn't be there to help her or address the issues at hand. I was trying to find a way to escape Taji and get home. This, of course, got me grounded from convoys and off of all missions. I only remember sitting outside of my room, headphones in and volume turned full blast, singing, and crying to Crazy Train. Not once, not twice, but on loop for hours on end. I'm gonna kill this guy that is messing with my daughter was the only thought in my head.

The Physical Stressors

There comes a time in your life when your brain thinks you can do something, but your body says otherwise. My time to start falling apart was at Camp Atterbury during our initial mobilization training. About six weeks before we flew overseas, I started having lung issues. I was placed on a no run profile that ended up getting extended every time it expired. A profile is a designation in the military that you are physically unable to perform certain tasks, and the profile paperwork is used as an excuse form. I guess when you get a bout of pneumonia and live in such 'clean conditions,' it's tough to recover from it.

One thing about the military. If there's no record of it then it didn't happen, and good luck trying to prove it afterwards.

Once we were in Al Taji, the physical problems started to compound. Of course, if you say anything and go to TMC (Troop Medical Clinic) you are considered a sick-call ranger. Now, a sick call ranger is one of those labels that you do not want in the military as it refers to a soldier that is just trying to get out of work by pretending to be sick.

That was a label that I wanted to avoid as did most other soldiers. So, how do you avoid the label? Keep quiet about your aches and pains. The knees were never meant to go sideways. This is a fairly common occurrence when you are trying to walk in sand while wearing 100 pounds of body armor. And your neck? It isn't supposed to get compressed from wearing a helmet, night vision goggles, and regular goggles for sand as it bounces while you are driving on the roads filled with potholes.

Dust storms were pretty bad in our area since Al Taji was the old chemical weapons manufacturing base for Saddam Hussein. The heavy metals left behind would be stirred up during the dust storms, so you had to stay inside until they were over.

The north side of the base, and one of the cities just across the river had wonderful burn pits that stunk to high heaven. Of course, we didn't know they were going to have lingering effects on any of us. It was all just part of deployment, right?

At the height of the problems, my feet, upper back, and side of my face were covered in sores. They were so bad that my t-shirt was constantly 'wet' from the seepage. I had to change my bed sheets daily due to them being soaked when I got up the next day. My feet got so bad that I couldn't wear my boots. The solution from the medics was to keep feeding me steroids. Every time I finished my round of meds the skin issue would reappear. To this day, I still don't know what led to my skin issues that I am still having.

Let's piece this all together if we can.

- I dealt with a younger private who tried to hurt himself. I spent about two weeks traveling back and forth with him.
- I started to have issues with my knees but didn't say anything to the medics.
- I began getting that undiagnosed rash on my body.
- I found out about my daughter's issues.
- We had to do a base-wide search for our staff sergeant who wanted to kill himself. Then I had to escort him to Germany (now my second trip there)
- While in Germany, I self-admitted to the hospital due to my skin disorder. My higher ups were less than thrilled with me about this move.

With all of these events happening, my mental ability was at its limit. I had nowhere to go and nobody to turn to for help. I started to wonder if God was really there with me. How could He allow all of this to happen? If things were going to be like this, then I didn't need or want Him in my life anymore. I can manage things myself.

It was during this time in my life that I turned my back on Jesus Christ because I didn't think He was really looking after me anyway. I decided I could manage my life all on my own.

The Realizations of Being Back Home

As I said earlier, I self-admitted into the hospital in Germany due to my skin disorder. This trip was at the end of our deployment and would cause me to miss the final convoy from Iraq back down to Kuwait. I was so mentally exhausted that I just didn't care anymore. After going through my medical appointments, I was put on a flight to Ft. Knox, Kentucky. All medical issues from a deployment go to Ft. Knox for further evaluations before being cleared to go to our regular homes.

Once I arrived at Ft. Knox, I began the process of clearing all medical protocols so I could be released back to my regular unit. My goal was to meet up with them at Camp Atterbury for our out processing, as I wanted to be able to go home on time, and with my unit, rather than staying at Ft. Knox for who knows how long....

During my stay at Ft. Knox, I had a weekend pass. Sharon jumped in her car and made the drive down to see me. I thought I was going to be excited to see her. To some extent, I was. I still couldn't process what I was feeling, let alone understanding why I felt the way that I do. Needless to say, she was still a welcome sight.

Sharon and I decided to get off of base for the day, so we made a trip to Mammoth Cave. This sounded like a great idea because we both loved to explore caves, take hikes, etc.. All of that outdoor stuff. This time was vastly different, and I was not expecting to react like I did.

It was nice getting out with Sharon. Getting away from the military way of life for a while was supposed to be refreshing. But, midway through the tour of the cave, I had my first of many panic attacks. It was dark, crowded, no visible exits, and some unruly children.

As I look back at this moment, I now see it as a foreshadowing of things that were to come with my blackouts and outbursts. I became so fixated on my surroundings that I froze in place and couldn't move or make any decisions. All I could do was hold Sharon's hand and let her lead me out like a little child. I could sure use a drink to help calm my nerves.

After 10 days of medical examinations and consultations, I was released to join up with the 1483rd at Camp Atterbury, IN for our company out processing so we could be released to our families back in Ohio.

Before we could be released from active duty and go back to our families, we spent days sitting in lines for mandatory safety briefs and medical screenings. We were checked for traumatic brain injury (TBI) and for our overall health. Many of the briefings were on either how to manage your finances, or who to call when you were struggling with suicidal thoughts.

Finally! After 11 months and 19 days of deployment, I'm back home with my wife and kids. Everything is back to normal, right? Not even close to normal.

Going to bed at night was extremely difficult. There were occasional nightmares, but the major issue was trying to share a bed with someone else again. I didn't want to be touched by anything other than the covers. Trying to deal with the quiet was simple. Put on the headphones and turn up the music so loud that you can't hear yourself think. This drove my wife nuts. She would ask me to turn it down and I would just look at her and turn it up louder.

I was really looking forward to using the extension of my orders for six weeks of pay after I returned home as a chance to 'recover.' I would lay on the couch watching ESPN all day long with my dog by my side. I would only get up for bathroom breaks, a cigarette, or refreshing my vodka. Sharon would force me to get out of the apartment with her for meals or to see family. I would reluctantly agree, but I was only there physically.

Prior to my deployment, I was working as a commercial union electrician. Two weeks after coming home, I got a call from work. They said they were really busy and asked if I would consider coming back to work sooner than expected. As I thought about it, I would be getting my federal pay and my normal pay? When do I start?

I worked about two weeks before issues really started to appear. I was not only argumentative with coworkers, but I had no drive to work hard. I was going through the motions. During this time, I was working in the Fairlawn area of Akron and had to drive one of the company bucket trucks to and from the shop to the job. On the way back to the shop, the smell of diesel fumes consumed my brain, and I was no longer in Akron. I was back in Iraq, driving through one of the shithole towns that always caused problems for us on our convoys. Once I regained my composure, I got the truck back to the shop, turned in the keys, and never drove it again.

The final straw for me in construction was while we were building a Kohl's store. I had already been back to work for a few weeks. It was definitely a struggle since I didn't want to really socialize with anybody. It also didn't help that I was still on edge and hyper vigilant. On this particular day, I was working on an electric platform lift in the ceiling when the flooring contractor threw a wood pallet onto the concrete floor behind me. Since the building was still just a shell, the sound was magnified. I was completely startled. Immediately, I was back in my truck watching the lead security truck getting hit by an IED.

I don't know how long I was out of it. It seemed like forever. Once I regained my whereabouts, I came down off of the lift, went outside and smoked three cigarettes to try and calm down. This was my last week in the trade, as I requested a voluntary layoff after this incident.

As I reflect back on these events, I think the outcome would have been the same whether I went back to work early or would have waited until I was off of federal orders.

I wasn't sure what I wanted to do now that I was in the midst of an unplanned career change. Life seems to throw you curve balls from time to time. Add into the equation a healthy dose of PTSD (that I was unaware of having at the moment), and you can really start to see how things could quickly spiral out of control.

I decided I would go back to school and get an associate degree in Business. Why not? I always wanted an office job. So, off to Fortis College for two years. Going back to school is pretty easy when you don't have to work. The classes weren't too overly difficult for me, so my drinking shouldn't be an issue, right?

Man, oh man. Put a 41-year-old man in a college full of early 20 something kids. The guys were annoying. The girls were beautiful. This could be a problem since I was still craving that adrenaline rush caused by being in Iraq. I had a fair amount of money saved up from the deployment, and Sharon was hoping to use it for bills and other household expenses, but I had other ideas. I could use it to keep getting my adrenaline rush.

During my last quarter of college, I had an internship with a minor league football team doing their marketing. Afternoons off, money to spend, opportunities to talk to pretty girls about being cheerleaders. What else could I ask for? But it still wasn't enough of an adrenaline rush. I had to find another place to find pretty girls for tryouts. Let's go to the dancer bars on the outskirts of town on a regular basis. Now, I never said I was thinking in my right mind yet.

The oddest part about all of this was the fact that never once had I quit loving my wife or thinking she was beautiful and the love of my life. I just needed to get the adrenaline fix again, and again...

The only thing that came out of my frequent trips to the dancer bars was getting drunk and not having any more money. Now, what else can I do to feel complete again?

Sharon has always trusted me. Even through my drive for adrenaline, deep in my heart I never wanted to ruin her trust in me. There were so many of these things that I did that I think she didn't know about, but I'm pretty certain now that she had an idea of what I was doing. She never stopped praying for me or loving me.

I tried to continue acting the part of a normal civilian for months after coming home. It's now October of 2010 and Sharon, Dylan and I were driving through downtown Kent, OH during the annual Kent State University Halloween party. This event is always a site to behold as the college kids trek from the dorms to the downtown bars in their costumes.

Now, traffic was particularly bad this evening and my road rage was beginning to flare up. As I was white knuckling the steering wheel, trying to find a way out of this chaos, I found an empty parking lot to pull into and gather myself. I parked the car, got out, and went and sat under a parking lot light. At this time, I completely forgot that I had others in the car with me.

Sharon came up behind me to check on me. This was the only time in my life that I almost hit her. The poor girl. She didn't know to not come up behind me quietly and unannounced and grab my shoulder. It was at this very moment that I realized that I needed to talk to a professional. I could never forgive myself if I hurt my wife or kids.

Part of the deal of my promotion to staff sergeant while I was in Iraq was that it required me to change units again when I got home. So, in October 2010, I was attached to my new unit, the 1486th Transportation Company in Mansfield, OH.

One of the unique things with the Army National Guard is that you will have soldiers attached to a deploying unit that are from other sister units. I was from the 1484th. There were others from the 1485th,1486th, and 1487th that also went with us. Sergeant Delaney (JD) was from the 86th.

JD was one of those laid back, younger sergeants that really hit it off with his age group. During our deployment, people would stop by his room on a regular basis for encouragement, or just to get things off of their chests. In October of 2010, before our next monthly drill in Mansfield, Sgt. John Delaney lost his battle with PTSD.

What a sobering moment for many of us. How could this happen? Especially to JD? It still hurts to think about it as I write about this event. I will never get out of my mind the picture of his distraught family as we all showed up in our Class A dress uniforms to pay our last respects. Is this my fate? I better get another drink, so I won't have to think about it.

I didn't realize how bad I was getting. Between the drinking, being unproductive, and not seeking help with the VA, I was causing major unspoken issues with Sharon and my son Dylan.

Now, up to this point of my time home, Sharon continued to encourage me to go to church with her. I reluctantly went with her but was more there physically than emotionally. Since I was already struggling with not wanting anything to do with Christ, all of the unimportant things at the church really annoyed me.

The entire time that I was gone, the church family was more worried about me than they were Sharon or the kids. Nobody reached out to them to see if they needed any help of any kind. Once I was home, the feeling was that I was back and there was nothing else that needed done. I got to the point to where I even shared one Sunday morning about our deployment. The one response that stuck in my head was from this sweet old lady who asked me if I was glad to be home from my mission's trip.

Seriously? I spent close to a year in a combat zone, and you think I was on a mission's trip? I don't need these God people! (Or so I thought)

In her solitude in the evenings of my deployment, Sharon found an online church that was local. It turned out that the lead pastor happened to be the son of a pastor we had previously at our old church. After my return home, Sharon decided that she wanted us to try out this new church. Reluctantly, I went with her.

Now, as all of this was happening, I was still in school and doing my thing. School in the morning, bars in the afternoon, watching television in the evening. Lather, rinse, repeat. I was a regular at a local sports bar by now and they would line up my shots for me when I sat down at the bar. I didn't even have to order anything. They knew what to do. Four drinks to start, two more, than singles after that until I couldn't think anymore. The struggle of coming home was very real to me at this point.

Our local Veteran's Service Commission (VSC) was a Godsend though I didn't realize it at the moment. They helped me to navigate the VA and the process to go through compensation and pension (comp. and pen. as we would call it in the military). As I was being evaluated for my skin disorder, the doctors started asking me other questions in regard to my deployment.

Questions like, do you feel hopeless? Have you ever thought of hurting yourself? Have you had dreams that wake you up at night? Do you have trust issues? Odd questions to ask for a skin disorder was my thought. It turns out that the VSC also submitted me for evaluation of PTSD due to being overseas and for the episodes of being a psych patient escort.

While I was still going to school, it was part of my responsibility to pick up Dylan from school on certain afternoons. Streetsboro Middle School was on campus with the high school, and they shared a common road. In the afternoons, they would have a gate pulled for traffic flow. Well, it was inconvenient for me, and I would always go around it. Except for this one day when another parent was stopped in the road going the correct direction and I couldn't get around the gate. I politely honked my horn and motioned for him to move forward. The response was a 'no,' and I didn't like that answer.

I don't remember getting out of the car that day, but Dylan and his best friend said I got out and charged the other car while swearing heavily at him. He must have gotten scared because he moved. The fact that I had blacked out and got aggressive in front of children shook me to the core. I needed another drink.

Here's the thing, when you drive overseas in convoys, you are always on the lookout for roadside bombs, hidden insurgents on or under bypasses, or anything out of the ordinary. Because we were the biggest vehicles on the road, you learned to stay aggressive so that you didn't get stopped in any type of a choke point that could result in an ambush. That driving style doesn't translate well to civilian driving.

It's not ok to get aggressive with other drivers when you're behind the wheel of a car. They call that 'road rage,' and I had a great deal of it at this time. Nobody liked riding with me. I would veer off of an exit ramp to chase someone down that was still on the highway, or I would try to run them off of the road if they innocently changed lanes in front of me when I felt that they should have stayed in their own lane.

One other time at the high school campus, a teenager decided to blow through the stop sign and pull out in front of me. Again, I had Dylan and friends in the car. Once again, I blacked out with rage. I came to when I was standing outside of the young man's car at the next stop sign. Poor Dylan, what must his friends be thinking of his psychotic dad? Damn, I need another drink.

If things weren't bad enough with the road rage, the drinking was about to get to another level. In early 2011, I received a call that one of my best friends from our unit in Iraq had died of a lung disease. No! Not Sean! Why Sean?! First JD, and now Sean! I can't take this anymore.

I stormed out of the apartment and went to find a movie at the local video store. I saw the movie 'Fracture' on a flight and liked the plot, so I wanted to see it again. It would be a great distraction for me. Needless to say, it wasn't available. So, instead, I bought another bottle of vodka and headed home.

By the time Sharon came home around 6pm, I had drunk the entire bottle and was curled up in the fetal position sobbing like a baby. "They didn't have the f____ movie I wanted at the store! And Sean's gone!" Sharon didn't know whether to laugh at my drunken state or to cry about my reactions. I sure put her through a lot of hell during this time of my life.

Since I was still in school when all of this happened with Sean, I went in the next morning, still drunk, and announced to my peers that I was struggling due to the sudden death of a friend. Have you ever been around someone that is what I would call a 'one-upper'? No matter what you are experiencing, they have had it worse. This was the wrong time for this lady to chime in. I think I might have called her a few choice words and went about my business. Yep, you guessed it, I needed another drink.

Now Sean Saricca was from my original unit, the 1484th, before I reenlisted. He had eventually transferred full time to the 1483rd before I got there. He and I hit it off immediately. He took me under his wing and helped me get acclimated to the new unit and to introduce me to others that he thought I would mesh with. He was a close friend. God, I miss him to this day.

Speaking of God, I was so angry at Him now. First it was JD, now it was Sean. God, you sure aren't doing me any favors here, so why should I concern myself with you? The emptiness and hollowness that I felt deep down in my soul was real, but I hurt too much to acknowledge what could actually heal me. So, I turned back to the bottle.

Sharon was starting to tire of the drinking and me wasting money. I could sense it. I didn't want to be touched. I didn't want to talk about how I felt. Headphones on at night with music blasting while I slept helped to drown out my thoughts. I was truly hurting.

I was so surprised to see a letter of declaration from the VA stating that I was awarded a 70% disability rating. I could now seek treatment without any out-of-pocket expenses. My first trip to the mental building (that's what I like to call the psych department) was both good and bad. I was assigned a nurse practitioner who was a veteran of the Gulf War. He understood me. The actual Dr. that I was to see was of Arab descent, and never served in the military. That was enough for me to never go back to him. Boy, was I ever messed up in my thinking processes?

Mr. Benson, my NPN, prescribed me some medications. One of them was to help me sleep with no nightmares or intrusive thoughts. It was a really, really good sleeping aid. Almost too good. If I couldn't get through all of this, maybe I could take a bunch of my pills. Who cares if I don't ever wake up?

I remember a time when I was having another one of my rough nights. Sharon wasn't happy with me. I wasn't happy with me. I was emotionally tired. I went outside to smoke a couple of cigarettes, but when I flicked the butt with the lit end as I finished, I started thinking about the tracers going back and forth the night that our convoy was stopped due to the lead truck getting hit by an IED.

I remembered that there was a magnet on our refrigerator from the military. It was for a talk line. I could sure use someone to talk to, so I called. What I didn't realize is that it was actually a suicide prevention hotline. I'm not too sure what all we discussed, but the next day, I got a call from the mental building wanting me and Sharon to come in to talk about the previous night. I don't know if I can trust this VA system. They won't let me just vent. Oh, how many distorted thoughts went through my mind at this time.

I was so frustrated. The only people that I felt that I could trust were the bartenders at my local watering hole. They understood me, as they kept my shot glasses full. They kept my mind from thinking. But my heart and soul were still empty.

Throughout all of this, Sharon never gave up on me. She always prayed for me and encouraged me to go to church with her. I would go at times just to keep her happy. It was at about this time that she decided that she wanted to go to the church that she had been listening to online. I wasn't sure about the changes, especially since I didn't want anything else to do with God.

When we first walked into Hudson Community Chapel, I was on full alert. The crowd was too much to bear. I would wait until the crowd died down before I would enter the church and make a beeline right for the sanctuary. Sharon agreed to sit where I was most comfortable. That would be the very last row of pews and with the door in site.

I sat down in the pew and didn't move. I didn't stand for worship; I didn't pray during prayer. I sat with my arms crossed and very guarded. Why would I want to communicate with a God that I felt abandoned me while I was in some of the most dangerous moments of my life?

One of the most paralyzing feelings is getting overwhelmed in a large crowd. When the paralysis would hit, I wasn't able to think or process anything. Sharon would ask me which way I wanted to go, but I couldn't even answer that simple question.

I would get so bad that I would just hold on to Sharon's hand and she would have to lead me through the crowd. At other times, I would just bull my way through the crowds to get out as fast as possible, not caring if anyone were in my way.

Meanwhile, I completed my associate degree in Business and landed a job at Horton Archery. I was elated to work for a company that made crossbows. There was no better place locally for a veteran to work than somewhere that produced weapons. I never gave any thought to the transition that would come as I went from 20 years in construction, and a deployment overseas to an office job. I was definitely on the struggle-bus.

For me, the hardest transition from deployment to an office position was the whole chain of command in the offices. In Iraq, I had lots of responsibilities for lives and equipment. Now, in the civilian realm, I was the lowest-ranking person, but still had the mindset that I could be in charge.

It was also difficult transitioning from a culture of true accountability. When you are in the military, there are swift and decisive ramifications to not doing what you were told. In my mind, this did not (and still does not) exist in an office setting. Employees get away with doing things wrong, disobeying orders, not being responsible, and all with no punishment. This caused me to speak out in ways that didn't endear me to others in my office.

One example was when I had an angry customer up front who needed a warranty part for his bow. In the past couple of weeks, we were instructed in customer service to just go back and get the part because the parts manager was too busy. That's what I did on this day, only to get berated by a much younger employee, who also happened to be the warehouse manager. I didn't let him phase me and that made him angrier. By the time it was all said and done, I dressed him down with some very colorful vocabulary.

I was out of line since he was management and I was entry level, but that didn't matter to me. I was disrespected, so I was going to take swift action about that. Approximately 15 minutes later, I got an email from the C.O.O. asking me if this actually occurred. What really got me going were that the parts manager claimed that I said disparaging remarks about his wife who was the purchasing agent.

Here's the thing, if I do something wrong, I will be the first to admit it and take the blame for whatever I did. Likewise, if you accuse me of something that I did not do, I will not lay down and take it. I will push back. That is what I did in my response to the email. I told the C.O.O. that yes, I did berate the manager, but I never said anything about his wife. I also said that if he wanted to discuss this in person so we could look at the manager's history of how he treats others then I would be glad to meet with him. That was the end of it, and it was never brought up again. I was, though, asked to not talk to the warehouse manager unless absolutely necessary. No problem...

Unfortunately, Horton Archery had made some bad design decisions that caused them to shut their doors. I stayed with them until the final day. I was one of only six people that stayed until the end as I believe in loyalty. Sometimes to a fault.

I took the next few months taking my time looking for a job. I didn't want entry level, but I also didn't have the experience for anything else. This was very frustrating to me, but I pressed on and sent out more resumes. I honestly was in no hurry to find work since it was a beautiful summer.

During all of this time, I was seeing Mr. Bensen. He made sure that I was adjusting to my meds and starting to sleep soundly through the night. The music in the headphones didn't need to be so loud now, and that was a good thing.

After about 3 months of looking for work in 2012, I was offered a job with a local non-profit mental health agency. My job was to help others with their resumes and to teach them interviewing skills. This was an extremely rewarding position because I was making a difference in the lives of others. I also felt like I had some of that authority back in my daily routine. The drawback was that we partnered with state and local agencies for our referrals.

Remember earlier when I commented about not having the best office etiquette? Yes, this organization was stricter in their hierarchy than Horton, but there were still areas that were just as bad. Namely the liaison between our organization and the local agencies. She was a mean and spiteful human being.

People were scared of her and that allowed her to do whatever she wanted to whomever she wanted. Because I called her out in a meeting, she had it out for me. She even told me that she would make sure that I didn't succeed as she was not going to give me any referrals anymore. Therefore, setting me up to get fired for not meeting my quarterly goals.

This, obviously, didn't set well with me. We had a pretty big argument over this, and she had me so mad that all I could do was cry. If I didn't cry, I was going to hurt her and I knew that couldn't happen. When I went to my supervisor about her actions, I was told that is just how she is. Either she goes, or I go. This was my comment to upper management.

Three weeks later, I had a new position in the organization in a different department...

This was a blessing in disguise, and I didn't even know it at the time. God was looking after me and I was completely clueless to His hand at work.

I had accepted a position in the Operations Department doing purchasing and utility bill auditing. I wasn't sure about the position at first, but it fit me like a glove. I could do my job, not have to have a lot of social interaction, and know I was not going to have to answer for what others did. I was in charge of my own little area, and I loved it.

As with most jobs, the honeymoon phase wears out fairly quickly. We were starting to see quite a bit of turnover in our department. Little did I know, this was about to bring in some significant changes for my job description.

There was a new sheriff in town, and as the Operations Manager, she had a completely different vision for the department than her predecessor. Her ideas for streamlining the department were not met with much enthusiasm from our staff, but her ideas were really good. A little over ambitious, but really good. With the new direction of the operations team, we had to sign new job descriptions if we wanted to stay on board. I had nothing else lined up, so I had no real choice.

My new job description not only had me doing purchasing for the entire organization, but also added building maintenance on select buildings within the company and an additional duty with a contract for Custom and Border Patrol. One thing I have learned in life is that you do one thing and do it well.

During all of this turmoil at home and work, we were now firmly implanted into our church. I was starting to listen to the sermons and see how they were applying to my life again. I still didn't have much faith in God, as He was letting all of these things happen to me as He sat back with a smirk on His face (at least that was my interpretation). The enemy is good at warping thoughts.

As we started to become more regular attenders, we started to feel it was time to join a small community group within the church. A way to make the larger church feel a little smaller, and to get to know a few people a little more intimately. I was extremely nervous about the thought of trying to trust someone who didn't serve with me to help keep each other alive. But I knew I had to try it.

Our first two attempts at joining a community group were not good experiences. They didn't last for more than a few months. So, we decided to wait a while before trying again. A year later, we were introduced to a community group led by a guy named Jim. As it turned out, he was a former Captain in the Air Force. For once, I felt like there was someone at this church that would understand who I have become.

Jim and I really connected. This was the first man that I had truly trusted in many, many years. I felt as if I could confide in him with my deepest struggles and issues. He got me. Even with my struggles, he loved me and that made all of the difference. Jim loved me as unconditionally as any man could, and he helped me remember that Jesus loved me no matter what I have done or gone through. What is this warming sensation starting to burn inside of me? My heart was beginning to soften – finally.

As Jim continued leading this community group, he decided to have us read a book titled 'God Space' by Doug Pollock. In the first chapter, Pollock wrote about getting right with Christ before continuing in the book. I knew I was nowhere near where I needed to be in my walk with Jesus, as I still was keeping 'Christianity' at arm's length. That Wednesday night in February of 2016 was a night that I will always remember.

I tossed and turned throughout the night, thinking about the scripture that was discussed in chapter one of God Space. I couldn't sleep. I couldn't stop thinking. I began sobbing greatly and realized that it was the Holy Spirit once again convicting me. It was time to ask for forgiveness and come back to allowing Jesus to be Lord of my life. So, at 3:30am on that Wednesday night, I gave my life back to Christ.

The Tipping Point

The journey back has not been easy. Even as believer in Jesus Christ, I still have my struggles and inner demons. I sit here in 2021, wondering what is going wrong now. I can't put my finger on it, but I once again feel helpless. Apathetic. Uninspired. Ready to give up. I don't care about taking my meds. I'm wallowing in my own misery and once again liking it. All I want to do is not feel anymore.

These struggles are very real. Unfortunately, the collateral damage to those that I love is also very real. With not caring about anything, it is driving a wedge between me and Sharon. Why am I so mean to her? She does nothing but loves me unconditionally and I push her away. I find my comfort in the bottom of a bottle of bourbon anymore. I would much rather have a few drinks and not feel anything, than to process the struggles inside of me.

What is happening to me? When did I get so bad that I needed to drink daily? Is this solely from my deployment? Is this because I was a social drinker and liked what I drank on occasion? Are there any family members that suffer from alcohol abuse?

If it were from family history, then I have been like an ostrich with its head in the sand for most of my adult life.

I'm breaking down. If I'm not careful, I will ruin everything good in my life and not even care. But I will care, and I will more than likely end up doing something stupid if I don't get help again.

"Lord, I need you. I need you to heal me. I need you to take away the pain. As I sit here in tears, heart hurting, I beg for your forgiveness. I need to feel your love again. Please draw me back in so that I can feel your love. I'm sorry for how I have been treating Sharon. Please help me to be able to reconcile my marriage. Help me to put away my pride and ask for help from those that can give it to me. Amen"

Start of the Healing Process

As I prayed this prayer, I thought everything would be simply fine afterwards. Not the case. There was so much guilt and shame about how I was treating Sharon, so much disgust in looking at myself in the mirror every morning, so much inner turmoil that I was wrestling with about why I needed to drink so much. I don't have the answers. I don't want to think about it. I think I'll have another drink.

Sometimes life takes a funny turn, and you don't see it coming until it's too late. With the inner angst that I was feeling, I reached out to the VA to see if they could change my meds for PTSD. This *had* to be the issue as to why I was treating Sharon like I was. Well, I didn't like the answer that I received. The meds that I have been prescribed, are not only for PTSD but also for anger issues. The nurse practitioner recommended that I actually start counseling for my PTSD. Something I have refused to do since coming home in 2010.

Fast forward a week after the news from my nurse practitioner, and I have a teleconference scheduled with a VA psychiatrist (We'll call her Sheryl). I hate talking about my feelings. I don't need this. It will be a waste of my time. You name it, I used it as a reason as to why I didn't need help. Sheryl was different in her approach than the other Dr. that I tried 10 years ago. Was it me that changed? I don't know, and I guess it really doesn't matter at this point.

She began asking me the standard PTSD questions. Have you been sleeping ok? Do you feel down? Have you thought about hurting yourself or anyone else? Do you drink alcohol?

My answers were "No. No. No. Yes." Sheryl decided to probe a little more into my drinking habits. This was more difficult than I imagined it would be, as it opened the floodgates of guilt and shame about my continued drinking and helplessness to stop. I also broke down over how much I was verbally hurting my wife. She didn't deserve to be treated this way.

After being questioned for what felt like an eternity, Sheryl had two conclusions that she wanted to review. "First, let's look at some better coping strategies. But, if we are going to look at these strategies, we need to rule out a substance use disorder (SUD)." WHAT? I'm not an addict! What is she saying? I just enjoy my bourbon!

In my mind, I decided that I would take the assessment for SUD so that I could prove everyone wrong about their assumptions of me. Boy, was this something that blew up in my face. I went to the VA in Akron, OH for my assessment. It felt a little awkward going in since I didn't have a 'problem,' but the guy doing the assessment (Damian) was really nice. We talked for about an hour.

After we were done talking, he told me that he determined that I do, in fact, have a substance use disorder. How did he know that? We only talked. Well, it turns out that the talking was him actually incorporating the DSM-5 (a comprehensive questionnaire for disorders) into our conversation.

"How bad is it?," I asked. Fully expecting to hear that it wasn't so bad. The response that I got shook me to my core. "The evaluation for substance use disorder rates in three categories. Mild (answering 'yes' to less than three questions), moderate (answering 'yes' to up to five questions), and severe (answering 'yes' to six or more questions). You were well above the six, so you are being diagnosed with a severe substance use disorder.

I was crushed. I planned to go in and prove to everyone that I had my drinking under control, but deep down inside, I knew there was a problem. I called Sharon immediately after the assessment and told her what was said. I knew her response, but it was so comforting to hear her say the words "You know I'll be right by your side through all of this."

How do I get to where I don't want to drink every night? Is it even possible to no longer drink every night? Where do I go from here? I was given two options. The first was complete abstinence. The second was to learn how to get my drinking under control.

My initial thought was, "There's no way I can even go 24 hours without a drink, and you want me to give it up completely?" This thought frightened me. I love my alcohol. I'll miss it too much. What do I do with myself in the evenings? Man, I need a drink!

My obvious choice from the two options was to learn how to control my drinking. As we talked in Damian's office, he eventually told me that most people that are as severe as I am end up back in his office within a year when not going completely abstinent. "Fine. I'll try this approach if it keeps me out of your office. Now, what do I have to do? I'm scared."

There were many things going on in my life at church, and it got me thinking. How will this affect my ability to serve? Will I still be allowed to serve? I need to call my Pastor.

I was so happy to talk to one of our pastoral staff after the diagnosis. As we talked, it was a mutual agreement that I take a break from leading a small group Bible study so that I could heal myself and my marriage. The first question Ken asked me (yes, we have the same first name) was about how Sharon is doing through all of this.

Then it hit me – I'm a Deacon in our church. What does all of this do for my standing as a Deacon?

The Bible clearly states the requirements to be a Deacon in any Bible believing church. 1 Timothy 3:8 (NIV) states "In the same way, deacons are to be worthy of respect, sincere, not indulging in much wine, and not pursuing dishonest gain."

It's amazing how, when you are at your rock bottom, that the enemy likes to put thoughts in your head of uncertainty, like the church doesn't really care about me. They're just going to kick me out. Nobody there loves me. Total nonsense!

Prior to a meeting that was scheduled with our acting lead Pastor (our current lead Pastor was on sabbatical), Zach came up to me between services and put his arm around me. "You know," he said, "when a soldier is wounded in battle, you don't kick him out of the Army. You pull him off of the front lines and help him heal."

What words of encouragement to hear during one of the lowest points in my life. The church cares about me. They care about my family. I am genuinely loved.

Due to my work schedule, I had to be outsourced to a contractor for the VA. It turns out that it was through Summa Health, and less than a mile from where I live. IOP (Intensive Outpatient Program) goes on for a minimum of 16 meetings. That's three nights per week for three hours a night. It's definitely hard to drink when you're at a meeting every night.

I went in for my intake assessment and answered all of the questions again. Why couldn't they use my assessment from the VA? I hate talking about this stuff with people. Especially when I don't feel like I truly have a problem. I just drink too much. I'm not an alcoholic.

The first meeting was, shall I say, interesting. There weren't many people in the meeting. I had to introduce myself with "My name is Ken and I'm an alcoholic." I didn't believe this, but I had to follow the rules. Since I was so guarded, I critiqued everything that happened in that three hours. I went home and told Sharon that it was 'stupid' and that I'm not going to go back.

I promised Sharon and my mentor from church that I would give it one more shot. I'm glad that I did. I have learned so much about myself and what this disease does to the brain (I'll leave those detailed facts to the professionals). Needless to say, I have learned that a switch has flipped, and I can no longer drink any alcohol without trying to believe one small lie and one big lie.

The small lie is that I can manage only having one drink. The big lie is telling myself that I won't ever do it again.

I am currently involved in AA and a recovery group at our church. I am finding that personal acceptance of my disease is the hardest thing for me to do at this time. It's one thing for someone to tell you you're an alcoholic, but I needed to come to the realization myself that I have a problem.

This realization did not occur until Christmas Eve of 2021. For a week leading up to this event, I had already been planning to buy a bottle of bourbon to drink. "I've gone since the end of July without a drink, so I should be well enough to manage one drink." The small lie crept in, and I didn't even know it.

Since Christmas Eve was a holiday from work this year, I decided to do some cooking for the holiday. What a perfect time to get a bottle! I can go home from shopping, go to Christmas Eve service, then come home and have a pour (only one of course). Things did not go as planned.

I have been told for months to reach out to my sponsor in AA or another member when the thought of drinking happens. It's amazing how difficult it is to pick up that phone. My pride wouldn't let me. I remember even telling myself, "No, I don't want to call. I am going to do this." Premeditated, and stupid now that I look back.

Sharon had to work on Christmas Eve, so we decided to just meet up at church for service. As she was getting me caught up on her day, she shared her struggles with all of the sweets that were brought into her work. I listened, but not with the intent of being a support for her. I listened so I could have more of an excuse to actually open the bottle that I purchased earlier in the day.

When we got home from church, Sharon saw the bottle and asked who it was for. I was always a brazen drinker and not afraid of what others said or thought. So, I told her it was mine, and that if she could struggle with the sweets at work, then I could have a drink if I wanted. The accusations were false and also extremely damaging.

As I heard myself spewing these webs of lies, I felt increasingly guilty. I poured my first drink and sat down in my chair. I looked over at Sharon on the love seat, she was trying not to cry. So, I drank the bourbon to ease the guilt. I looked over again and she was crying. Now I'm mad at myself, so I think I'll have another drink.

At this point, she was sobbing on the couch. I was so angry, and guilt ridden now that I decided to have another drink. Not one drink. Not two drinks, but half of the bottle- again. Poor Sharon. What did I do? Why did I say that?

She gathered her composure enough to tell me that she can't do this anymore. She cannot be held responsible for my sobriety. With this, she went up to bed. Leaving me to wallow in the mess that I made.

More guilt popped up, and more alcohol was consumed until I was ready to pass out in bed. The only thought I remember is "Why am I doing this again?"

One of the hardest things for me to do at times is to tell someone close to me that I was wrong. This was an instance to where I had to make sure that my apology was sincere. On Christmas Day, I asked Sharon for forgiveness, explaining that I had already purchased the bourbon before I knew about her day. The events of her day were nothing but an excuse for me to open up the bottle.

Reflecting back on the weeks leading up to this event, I see how arrogant and prideful I had become. It had all become about me.

How many days sober. Who is going to ask me how I am doing so that I can tell them how wonderful things are going. Pride. Puffed up. Arrogant. Call it what you want, but that was me.

Getting humbled is, well, a humbling experience. I am just so thankful that we have such a loving and compassionate God who shows us grace and mercy.

This experience has taught me that I do have a disease and cannot drink any alcohol without severe consequences.

To admit that you are truly powerless over something is difficult. This is a path that I will be walking for the rest of my life. I won't be walking alone. If I am to stay the course, I need to rely solely on my faith in Christ and submit to His will daily.

The support from family and friends has been unbelievable. I want to thank all of you for your love, prayers, and kindness. I will continue to do everything in my power to honor Jesus in my journey as I cannot do this without His help.

Made in the USA
Middletown, DE
05 May 2022